Sarah Daniel

AIR FRYER
CAKES & BAKES
VOL. 1

Sweet, mouthwatering treats for the family!

Kensington Recipe Press

Photography Humbert Castillo
Graphic design Yuka Okuma
Editorial coordination Lizzie Martin

First edition March 2021

Table of Contents

Introduction

Sarah Daniel is a passionate cookbook writer with over two decades of professional culinary expertise. Known for her culinary skills and high standard, she has combined her classic recipes tailored to use with the modern cooking appliance in her new cookbook series "The Complete Air Fryer Cookbook" for Kensington Recipe Press. She loves to employ innovations in cooking by keeping the traditional elements and richness.

We can always find the art of simplicity in her recipes, making her a step ahead of many innovative cooking methods. All of her books include self-tested recipes, and the pleasure of sharing exciting experiments is evident in most of her recipe works.

Popularly known as a "recipe development whiz" among her circle, she contributes recipes to several reputed magazines. She helps you discover something new and impressive. Beyond her books, she maintains a strong influence among her friends and family as an enthusiast of healthy eating and living.

Having spent considerable time writing the series "The Complete Air Fryer Cookbook", Sarah has carefully penned her research with super versatile meal ideas without compromising quality and nutritional values. Her approach to modern food tech is mind-blowing.
This Cookbook Series is a pioneering endeavor blended with modern cooking with traditional values by focusing on healthy, balanced food. It is a reference series for people who love having healthy food.

Cakes & Bakes

Angel Food Cake

Ready about in: 30 min | Serves 12 | Normal

Ingredients

¼ cup butter, melted

1 cup powdered erythritol

1 teaspoon strawberry extract

12 egg whites

2 teaspoons cream of tartar

A pinch of salt

Directions:

Select bake mode the set the temperature to preheat the Air Fryer for 5 minutes.

Mix the egg whites and cream of tartar.

Use a hand mixer and whisk until white and fluffy.

Add the rest of the ingredients except for the butter and whisk for another minute.

Pour into a baking dish.

Place in the Air Fryer basket and cook for 30 minutes at 400° F or if a toothpick inserted in the middle comes out clean.

Drizzle with melted butter once cooled.

Serve and Enjoy

Vanilla Pound Cake

Ready about in: 30 min | Serves 12 | Easy

Ingredients

¼ teaspoon salt

½ cup erythritol powder

1 vanilla bean, scraped

1/3 cup water

2/3 cup butter, melted

4 large eggs

Directions:

Select bake mode the set the temperature to preheat the Air Fryer for 5 minutes.

Combine all ingredients in a mixing bowl.

Pour into a greased baking dish.

Bake in the Air Fryer for 30 minutes at 3750° F.

When the timer reaches 0, then press the cancel button

Serve and Enjoy

Chia Pudding

Ready about in: 10 min | Servings: 1 | Easy

Ingredients

cup chia seeds

1 cup unsweetened coconut milk

1 teaspoon liquid Sugar

1 tablespoon coconut oil

1 teaspoon Butter

Directions:

Select bake mode the set the temperature to preheat the Air Fryer at 360° F.

In a bowl, gently combine the chia seeds with the milk and Sugar before mixing the coconut oil and butter. Spoon seven equal-sized portions into seven ramekins and set these inside the Fryer.

Cook for 4 minutes. Take care when removing the ramekins from the Fryer and allow to cool for 4 minutes.

When the timer reaches 0, then press the cancel button

Serve and Enjoy

Banana-Choco Brownies

Ready about in: 30 min | Serves 12 | Easy

Ingredients

2 cups almond flour

2 teaspoons baking powder

½ teaspoon baking powder

½ teaspoon baking soda

½ teaspoon salt

1 over-ripe banana

3 large eggs

½ teaspoon stevia powder

¼ cup coconut oil

1 tablespoon vinegar

1/3 cup almond flour

1/3 cup cocoa powder

Directions:

Select bake mode the set the temperature to preheat the Air Fryer for 5 minutes.

Combine all ingredients in a food processor and pulse until well-combined.

Pour into a baking dish that will fit in the Air Fryer.

Place in the Air Fryer basket and cook for 30 minutes at 350° F or if a toothpick inserted in the middle comes out clean.

When the timer reaches 0, then press the cancel button

Serve and Enjoy

Churros

Ready about in: 15 min | Servings: 1 | Easy

Ingredients

½ cup water

¼ cup butter

½ cup flour

3 eggs

2 ½ teaspoon sugar

Directions:

In a saucepan, bring the water and butter to a boil. Once it is bubbling, add the flour and mix to create a doughy consistency.

Remove from the heat, allow to cool, and crack the eggs into the saucepan. Blend with a hand mixer until the dough turns fluffy.

Transfer the dough into a piping bag.

Select bake mode the set the temperature to preheat the Air Fryer at 380° F.

Pipe the dough into the Fryer in several three-inch-long segments. Cook for 10 minutes before removing from the Fryer and coating in the Sugar.

Serve with the low-carb chocolate sauce of your choice.

Hazelnut Brownie Cups

Ready about in: 30 min | Servings: 12 | Normal

Ingredients

6 ounce semisweet chocolate chips

1 stick butter, at room temperature

1 cup sugar

2 large eggs

¼ cup red wine

¼ teaspoon hazelnut extract

1 teaspoon pure vanilla extract

¾ cup flour

2 tablespoon cocoa powder

½ cup ground hazelnuts

Pinch of kosher salt

Directions:

Melt the butter and chocolate chips in the microwave.

In a large bowl, combine the Sugar, eggs, red wine, hazelnut and vanilla extract with a whisk. Pour in the chocolate mix.

Add in the flour, cocoa powder, ground hazelnuts, and a pinch of kosher salt, continuing to stir until a creamy, smooth consistency is achieved.

Take a muffin tin and place a cupcake liner in each cup. Spoon an equal amount of the batter into each one.

Air bake at 360° F for 28 - 30 minutes, cooking in batches if necessary.

Serve with a topping of ganache if desired.

Apple-Toffee Upside-Down Cake

Ready about in: 30 min | Serves 9 | Normal

Ingredients

¼ cup almond butter

¼ cup sunflower oil

½ cup walnuts, chopped

¾ cup + 3 tablespoon coconut sugar

¾ cup water

1 ½ teaspoon mixed spice

1 cup plain flour

1 lemon, zest

1 teaspoon baking soda

3 baking apples, cored and sliced

Directions:

Select bake mode the set the temperature to preheat the Air Fryer to 390° F.

In a skillet, melt the almond butter and 3 tablespoons sugar. Pour the mixture over a baking dish that will fit in the Air Fryer. Arrange the slices of apples on top. Set aside.

In a mixing bowl, combine flour, ¾ cup sugar, and baking soda. Add the mixed spice.

In another bowl, mix the oil, water, vinegar, and lemon zest. Stir in the chopped walnuts. Combine the wet ingredients to the dry ingredients until well combined. Pour over the tin with apple slices. Bake for 30 minutes or until a toothpick inserted comes out clean.

White Chocolate Berry Cheesecake

Ready about in: 45-50 min | Servings: 4 | Easy

Ingredients

8 ounce cream cheese, softened

2 ounce heavy cream

1 1/4 cups graham cracker crumbs

2 tablespoons sugar

1 tablespoon cornstarch

1/2 cup water

1/4 cup butter, melted

2 cups white chocolate chips

1 teaspoon raspberry

3 (8 oz.) packages cream cheese, softened

1/2 cup sugar

1 tablespoon flour

2 eggs, room temperature

1 teaspoon vanilla

Directions:

In a medium bowl, mix together graham cracker crumbs and melted butter

In a medium saucepan, make the raspberry sauce by combining raspberries, 2 tablespoons sugar, cornstarch, and water.

Select bake mode the set the temperature to preheat oven Air Fryer to 325° F

In a metal bowl over a pan of simmering water, melt white chocolate chips, occasionally stirring until smooth.

Place a baking pan filled with hot water on the lower rack of the oven. In a large bowl, beat cream cheese and 1/2 cup sugar with an electric mixer until smooth. With the mixer on low speed, blend in eggs one at a time. Blend in vanilla and melted white chocolate.

Spoon 3 tablespoons raspberry sauce over batter. Pour remaining cheesecake batter into pan, and again spoon 3 tablespoons raspberry sauce over the top

Bake for 45 to 50 minutes, or until filling is set and refrigerate for 6 hours before removing from pan.

Serve with remaining raspberry sauce.

Blueberry & Lemon Cake

Ready about in: 17 min | Serves 4 | Normal

Ingredients

2 eggs

1 cup blueberries

zest from 1 lemon

juice from 1 lemon

1 teaspoon vanilla

brown sugar for topping (a little sprinkling on top of each muffin-less than a teaspoon)

2 1/2 cups self-rising flour

1/2 cup Monk Fruit (or use your preferred sugar)

1/2 cup cream

1/4 cup avocado oil (any light cooking oil)

Directions:

In mixing bowl, beat well wet Ingredients. Stir in dry ingredients and mix thoroughly.

Lightly grease baking pan of Air Fryer with cooking spray. Pour in batter.

For 12 minutes, cook on 330° F.

When setting a cooking time less than 20 minutes, first set the cooking time to 20 minutes.

Then, turn the time/darkness control knob to the desired cooking time

Let it stand in Air Fryer for 5 minutes.

When the timer reaches 0, then press the cancel button

Easy Baked Chocolate Mug Cake

Ready about in: 15 min | Serves 3 | Normal

Ingredients

½ cup cocoa powder

½ cup stevia powder

1 cup coconut cream

1 package cream cheese, room temperature

1 tablespoon vanilla extract

4 tablespoons butter

Directions:

Select bake mode the set the temperature to preheat the Air Fryer for 5 minutes.

In a mixing bowl, combine all ingredients.

Use a hand mixer to mix everything until fluffy.

Pour into greased mugs.

Place the mugs in the Fryer basket.

Bake for 15 minutes at 350° F.

Place in the fridge to chill before serving.

Chocolate Cheesecake

Ready about in: 60 min | Servings: 4 | Easy

Ingredients

4 ounce cream cheese

½ ounce heavy cream

1 cup crushed chocolate wafer crumbs

3 tablespoons butter, melted

1 teaspoon Sugar Glycerite

1 ounce Enjoy Life mini chocolate chips

FILLING:

4 ounce cream cheese

½ ounce heavy cream

2 tablespoons all-purpose flour

2 large eggs, room temperature

1 teaspoon vanilla extract

Instructions

In a small bowl, combine cookie crumbs and Sugar; stir in butter.

Combine all the ingredients except the chocolate to a thick consistency.

Bake at 350° F for 40-45 minutes or until the center is almost set.

 Cool on a wire rack for 10 minutes. Carefully run a knife around the edge of the pan to loosen; cool 1 hour longer. Refrigerate in serving cups.

Garnish slices with strawberries and chocolate shavings if desired.

Fold in the chocolate chips.

Refrigerate in serving cups.

Crust

Ready about in: 60 min | Servings: 3 | Easy

Ingredients

2 cups flour

4 teaspoon melted butter

1 teaspoon sugar.

2 large eggs

½ teaspoon salt

7 Tablespoons ice water.

8 Tablespoons all-vegetable shortening

Instructions

Place one of the rolled out dough circles into a pie plate, pinching the edges to form a crust

Place the crust in the freezer for at least 30 minutes

Mix together the flour and butter.

Add in the eggs and salt and combine well to form a dough ball.

Preheat the oven Air Fryer to 375° F.

Cut a circle of parchment paper out as large as you rolled your crust

Bake the crust for 15 minutes. Remove the crust from the oven and remove the weights and the parchment paper

Place the crust back in the oven for an additional 10- 15 minutes until the crust is golden

Serve!

Vanilla Bean Dream

Ready about in: 35 min | Servings: 1 | Normal

Ingredients

½ cup extra virgin coconut oil, softened

½ cup coconut butter, softened

Juice of 1 lemon

Seeds from ½ a vanilla bean

Directions:

Whisk the ingredients in an easy-to-pour cup.

Pour into a lined cupcake or loaf pan. Reduce oven temperature to 325° F. Beat cream cheese in mixer bowl on medium-high speed for 3 minutes.

Refrigerate for 20 minutes. Top with lemon zest.

When the timer reaches 0, then press the cancel button

Serve!

Cherry-Choco Bars

Ready about in: 15 min | Serves 8 | Normal

Ingredients

¼ teaspoon salt

½ cup almonds, sliced

½ cup chia seeds

½ cup dark chocolate, chopped

½ cup dried cherries, chopped

½ cup prunes, pureed

½ cup quinoa, cooked

¾ cup almond butter

1/3 cup honey

2 cups old-fashioned oats

2 tablespoon coconut oil

Directions:

Select bake mode the set the temperature to preheat the Air Fryer to 375° F.

In a mixing bowl, combine the oats, quinoa, chia seeds, almond, cherries, and chocolate.

In a saucepan, heat the almond butter, honey, and coconut oil.

Pour the butter mixture over the dry mixture. Add salt and prunes. Mix until well combined.

Pour over a baking dish that can fit inside the Air Fryer.

Cook for 15 minutes.

Let it cool for 1 hour before slicing into bars.

Cherries 'n Almond Flour Bars

Ready about in: 35 min | Serves 12 | Difficult

Ingredients

¼ cup water

½ cup butter, softened

½ teaspoon salt

½ teaspoon vanilla

1 ½ cups almond flour

1 cup erythritol

1 cup fresh cherries, pitted

1 tablespoon xanthan gum

2 eggs

Directions:

In a mixing bowl, combine the first 6 ingredients until you form a dough.

Press the dough in a baking dish that will fit in the Air Fryer.

Place in the Air Fryer and bake for 10 minutes at 375° F.

Meanwhile, mix the cherries, water, and xanthan gum in a bowl.

Take the dough out and pour over the cherry mixture.

Return to the Air Fryer and cook for 25 minutes more at 375° F.

Chocolate Peanut Butter Cups

Ready about in: 70 min | Servings: 2 | Normal

Ingredients

1 stick unsalted butter

1 ounce cube unsweetened chocolate

5 packets Sugar in the Raw

1 tablespoon heavy cream

4 tablespoon peanut butter

Instructions

In a microwave, melt the butter and chocolate.

Add the Sugar.

Stir in the cream and peanut butter.

Stir peanut butter and powdered Sugar together until smooth.

Spread 1 to 2 tablespoons of chocolate in the bottom of each cupcake liner.

Dollop 1 to 2 teaspoons of the peanut butter mixture on top of the chocolate.

Line the muffin tins. Fill the muffin cups.

Freeze for 60 minutes or until chocolate has hardened.

Coco-Lime Bars

Ready about in: 20 min | Serves 3 | Easy

Ingredients

¼ cup almond flour

¼ cup coconut oil

¼ cup dried coconut flakes

¼ teaspoon salt

½ cup lime juice

¾ cup coconut flour

1 ¼ cup erythritol powder

1 tablespoon lime zest

4 eggs

Directions:

Select bake mode the set the temperature to preheat the Air Fryer for 5 minutes.

Combine all ingredients in a mixing bowl.

Place in greased mug.

Bake in the Air Fryer for 20 minutes at 375° F.

When the timer reaches 0, then press the cancel button

Serve and Enjoy

Coffee Flavored Doughnuts

Ready about in: 6 min | Serves 6 | Easy

Ingredients

¼ cup coconut sugar

¼ cup coffee

½ teaspoon salt

1 cup white all-purpose flour

1 tablespoon sunflower oil

1 teaspoon baking powder

2 tablespoon aquafaba

Directions:

In a mixing bowl mix together the dry Ingredients flour, sugar, salt, and baking powder.

In another bowl, combine the aquafaba, sunflower oil, and coffee.

Mix to form a dough.

Let the dough rest inside the fridge.

Select bake mode the set the temperature to preheat the Air Fryer to 400° F.

Knead the dough and create doughnuts.

Arrange inside the Air Fryer in single layer and cook for 6 minutes.

Do not shake so that the donut maintains its shape.

Serve and Enjoy

Choco-Peanut Mug Cake

Ready about in: 20 min | Serves 1 | Normal

Ingredients

¼ teaspoon baking powder

½ teaspoon vanilla extract

1 egg

1 tablespoon heavy cream

1 tablespoon peanut butter

1 teaspoon butter, softened

2 tablespoon erythritol

2 tablespoons cocoa powder, unsweetened

Directions:

Select bake mode the set the temperature to preheat the Air Fryer for 5 minutes.

Combine all ingredients in a mixing bowl.

Pour into a greased mug.

Place in the Air Fryer basket and cook for 20 minutes at 400° F or if a toothpick inserted in the middle comes out clean.

When the timer reaches 0, then press the cancel button

Serve and Enjoy

Macaroon Bites

Ready about in: 30 min | Servings: 2 | Easy

4 egg whites

½ teaspoon vanilla

½ teaspoon EZ-Sweet (or the equivalent of 1 cup artificial sweetener)

4½ teaspoon water

1 cup unsweetened coconut

Directions:

Select bake mode the set the temperature to preheat your Air Fryer to 375° F

Combine the egg whites, liquids and coconut.

Put into the Fryer and reduce the heat to 325° F

Bake for 15 minutes.

When the timer reaches 0, then press the cancel button

Serve!

Strawberry Shake

Ready about in: 5 min | Servings: 1 | Normal

Ingredients

3/4 cup coconut milk

¼ cup heavy cream

1 teaspoon vanilla extract

1 pint vanilla ice cream

7 ice cubes

2 tbsp sugar-free strawberry Torani syrup

¼ tsp Xanthan Gum

Directions:

Combine all the ingredients into a blender (the sliced strawberries, Sugar and vanilla)

Set aside and allow to macerate for at least 20 minutes and up to 1 hour

In a large mixer, place the strawberries, ice cream, and milk

Blend for 1-2 minutes.

Pour into ice cream parlor glasses and garnish the rim of each glass with whole strawberries.

Serve and Enjoy!

Coffee Flavored Cookie Dough

Ready about in: 20 min | Serves 12 | Normal

Ingredients

¼ cup butter

¼ teaspoon xanthan gum

½ teaspoon coffee espresso powder

½ teaspoon stevia powder

¾ cup almond flour

1 egg

1 teaspoon vanilla

1/3 cup sesame seeds

2 tablespoons cocoa powder

2 tablespoons cream cheese, softened

Instructions

Select bake mode the set the temperature to preheat the Air Fryer for 5 minutes.

Combine all ingredients in a mixing bowl.

Press into a baking dish that will fit in the Air Fryer.

Place in the Air Fryer basket and cook for 20 minutes at 400° F or if a toothpick inserted in the middle comes out clean.

When the timer reaches 0, then press the cancel button

Serve and Enjoy!

Cheesecake Cups

Ready about in: 10 min | Servings: 4 | Normal

Ingredients

8 ounce cream cheese, softened

3/4 cup graham cracker crumbs.

2 tablespoons salted butter, melted.

2 ounce heavy cream

1 teaspoon Sugar Glycerite

1 teaspoon Splenda

1 teaspoon vanilla flavoring (Frontier Organic)

Directions:

Combine all the ingredients.

Whip until a pudding consistency is achieved.

Divide into cups.

Refrigerate until served!

Enjoy!

Bread Pudding with Cranberry

Ready about in: 45 min | Serves 4 | Normal

Ingredients

1-1/2 cups milk

2-1/2 eggs

1/2 cup cranberries1 teaspoon butter

1/4 cup and 2 tablespoons white sugar

1/4 cup golden raisins

1/8 teaspoon ground cinnamon

3/4 cup heavy whipping cream

3/4 teaspoon lemon zest

3/4 teaspoon kosher salt

3/4 French baguettes, cut into 2-inch slices

3/8 vanilla bean, split and seeds scraped away

Directions:

Lightly grease baking pan of Air Fryer with cooking spray. Spread baguette slices, cranberries, and raisins.

In blender, blend well vanilla bean, cinnamon, salt, lemon zest, eggs, sugar, and cream. Pour over baguette slices. Let it soak for an hour.

Cover pan with foil.

For 35 minutes, cook on 330° F.

Let it rest for 10 minutes.

Serve and enjoy.

Coconutty Lemon Bars

Ready about in: 25 min | Serves 12 | Easy

Ingredients

¼ cup cashew

¼ cup fresh lemon juice, freshly squeezed

¾ cup coconut milk

¾ cup erythritol

1 cup desiccated coconut

1 teaspoon baking powder

2 eggs, beaten

2 tablespoons coconut oil

A dash of salt

Directions:

Select bake mode the set the temperature to preheat the Air Fryer for 5 minutes.

In a mixing bowl, combine all ingredients.

Use a hand mixer to mix everything.

Pour into a baking dish that will fit in the Air Fryer.

Bake for 25 minutes at 350° F or until a toothpick inserted in the middle comes out clean.

When the timer reaches 0, then press the cancel button

Serve and Enjoy!

Apple Pie in Air Fryer

Ready about in: 35 min | Serves 4 | Easy

Ingredients

½ teaspoon vanilla extract

1 beaten egg

1 large apple, chopped

1 Pillsbury Refrigerator pie crust

1 tablespoon butter

1 tablespoon ground cinnamon

1 tablespoon raw sugar

2 tablespoon sugar

2 teaspoons lemon juice

Baking spray

Directions:

Lightly grease baking pan of Air Fryer with cooking spray. Spread pie crust on bottom of pan up to the sides.

In a bowl, mix vanilla, sugar, cinnamon, lemon juice, and apples. Pour on top of pie crust. Top apples with butter slices.

Cover apples with the other pie crust. Pierce with knife the tops of pie.

Spread beaten egg on top of crust and sprinkle sugar.

Cover with foil.

For 25 minutes, cook on 390° F.

Remove foil cook for 10 minutes at 330° F until tops are browned.

Serve and enjoy.

Coffee 'n Blueberry Cake

Ready about in: 35 min | Serves 6 | Normal

Ingredients

1 cup white sugar

1 egg

1/2 cup butter, softened

1/2 cup fresh or frozen blueberries

1/2 cup sour cream

1/2 teaspoon baking powder

1/2 teaspoon ground cinnamon

1/2 teaspoon vanilla extract

1/4 cup brown sugar

1/4 cup chopped pecans

1/8 teaspoon salt

1-1/2 teaspoons confectioners' sugar for dusting

3/4 cup and 1 tablespoon all-purpose flour

Directions:

In a small bowl, whisk well pecans, cinnamon, and brown sugar.

In a blender, blend well all wet Ingredients. Add dry Ingredients except for confectioner's sugar and

blueberries. Blend well until smooth and creamy.

Lightly grease baking pan of Air Fryer with cooking spray.

Pour half of batter in pan. Sprinkle half of pecan mixture on top. Pour the remaining batter. And then topped with remaining pecan mixture. Cover pan with foil. For 35 minutes, cook on 330° F.

Serve and enjoy with a dusting of confectioner's sugar.

———

Pineapple Sticks

Ready about in: 20 min | Servings: 4 | Easy

Ingredients

½ fresh pineapple, cut into sticks

Toothpicks to serve

¼ cup desiccated coconut

Directions:

Select bake mode the set the temperature to preheat the Air Fryer to 400° F.

Coat the pineapple sticks in the desiccated coconut and put each one in the Air Fryer basket.

Air Fry for 10 minutes.

Place the pineapple chunk on top of the cheese chunk and skewer with the toothpick.

Serve immediately and Enjoy!

Chocolate Chip in a Mug

Ready about in: 20 min | Serves 6 | Easy

Ingredients

¼ cup walnuts, shelled and chopped

½ cup butter, unsalted

½ cup dark chocolate chips

½ cup erythritol

½ teaspoon baking soda

½ teaspoon salt

1 tablespoon vanilla extract

2 ½ cups almond flour

2 large eggs, beaten

Directions:

Select bake mode the set the temperature to preheat the Air Fryer for 5 minutes.

Combine all ingredients in a mixing bowl.

Place in greased mugs.

Bake in the Air Fryer for 20 minutes at 375° F.

When the timer reaches 0, then press the cancel button

Serve and Enjoy

Hot Coconut 'n Cocoa Buns

Ready about in: 8 min | Serves 8 | Normal

Ingredients

¼ cup cacao nibs

1 cup coconut milk

1/3 cup coconut flour

3 tablespoons cacao powder

4 eggs, beaten

Directions:

Select bake mode the set the temperature to preheat the Air Fryer for 5 minutes.

Combine all ingredients in a mixing bowl.

Form buns using your hands and place in a baking dish that will fit in the Air Fryer.

Bake for 15 minutes for 375° F.

Once Air Fryer turns off, leave the buns in the Air Fryer until it cools completely.

When the timer reaches 0, then press the cancel button

Serve and Enjoy

Crispy Good Peaches

Ready about in: 30 min | Serves 4 | Normal

Ingredients

1 teaspoon cinnamon

1 teaspoon sugar, white

1/3 cup oats, dry rolled

2 tablespoon Flour, white

3 tablespoon butter, unsalted

3 tablespoon pecans, chopped

4 cup sliced peaches, frozen

Directions:

Lightly grease baking pan of Air Fryer with cooking spray. Mix in a teaspoon cinnamon, 2 tablespoon flour, 3 tablespoon sugar, and peaches.

For 20 minutes, cook on 300° F.

Mix the rest of the Ingredients in a bowl. Pour over peaches.

Cook for 10 minutes at 330° F.

Serve and enjoy.

Coconut & Banana Cake

Ready about in: 1 hour 15 min | Servings: 5 | Normal

Ingredients

2/3 cup sugar, shaved

2/3 cup unsalted butter

3 eggs

1 ¼ cup flour

1 ripe banana, mashed

½ teaspoon vanilla extract

1/8 teaspoon baking soda

Sea salt to taste

Topping Ingredients

sugar to taste, shaved

Walnuts to taste, roughly chopped

Bananas to taste, sliced

Directions:

Select bake mode the set the temperature to preheat the Air Fryer to 360° F.

Mix together the flour, baking soda, and a pinch of sea salt.

In a separate bowl, combine the butter, vanilla extract and Sugar using an electric mixer or a blender, to achieve a fluffy consistency. Beat in the eggs one at a time.

Throw in half of the flour mixture and stir thoroughly. Add in the mashed banana and continue to mix. Lastly, throw in the remaining half of the flour mixture and combine until a smooth batter is formed. Transfer the batter to a baking tray and top with the banana slices.

Scatter the chopped walnuts on top before dusting with the Sugar

Place a sheet of foil over the tray and pierce several holes in it.

Put the covered tray in the Air Fryer. Cook for 48 minutes.

Decrease the temperature to 320° F, take off the foil, and cook for an additional 10 minutes until golden brown.

Insert a skewer or toothpick in the center of the cake. If it comes out clean, the cake is ready.

Strawberry Frozen Dessert

Ready about in: 45 minutes | Servings: 1 | Normal

Ingredients

½ cup sugar-free strawberry preserves

½ cup Sugar in the Raw or Splenda

2 cups Fage Total 0% Greek Yogurt

1 cup heavy whipping cream

3/4 cup unsalted butter, melted

3 cups graham cracker crumbs

Ice cream maker

Instructions

In a food processor, purée the strawberries. Add the strawberry preserves.

Combine graham cracker crumbs, Sugar and melted butter

Add the Greek yogurt and thoroughly mix.

After that beat cream cheese with powdered Sugar, at a low speed, until creamy, then add condensed milk, vanilla and pureed strawberries, until well combined.

Spread over the graham cracker layer

Leave in the freezer for at least 5 hours and take it out of the freezer about 20 – 30 minutes before serving.

Serve!

Swirled German Cake

Ready about in: 25 minutes | Servings: 8 | Easy

Ingredients

1 cup flour

1 teaspoon baking powder

1 cup sugar

1/8 teaspoon kosher salt

¼ teaspoon ground cinnamon

¼ teaspoon grated nutmeg

1 teaspoon orange zest

1 stick butter, melted

2 eggs

1 teaspoon pure vanilla extract

¼ cup milk

2 tablespoon unsweetened cocoa powder

Directions:

Take a round pan that is small enough to fit inside your Air Fryer and lightly grease the inside with oil.

In a bowl, use an electric mixer to combine the flour, baking powder, Sugar, salt, cinnamon, nutmeg, and orange zest.

Fold in the butter, eggs, vanilla, and milk, incorporating everything well.

Spoon a quarter-cup of the batter into the baking pan.

Stir the cocoa powder into the rest of the batter.

Use a spoon to drop small amounts of the brown batter into the white batter. Swirl them together with a knife.

Place the pan in the Air Fryer and cook at 360° F for about 15 minutes. Remove the pan from the Fryer and leave to cool for roughly 10 minutes.

Serve and Enjoy!

Choco-berry Fudge Sauce

Ready about in: 30 min | Servings: 2 | Easy

Ingredients

4 ounce cream cheese, softened

1-3.5 ounce 90% chocolate Lindt bar, chopped

¼ cup powdered erythritol

¼ cup heavy cream

1 tablespoon Monin sugar-free raspberry syrup

Directions:

In a large skillet, melt together the cream cheese and chocolate.

Stir in the sweetener.

Remove from the heat and allow to cool.

Once cool, mix in the cream and syrup.

Serve and Enjoy!

Berry Layer Cake

Ready about in: 8 min | Servings: 1 | Easy

Ingredients

¼ lemon pound cake

¼ cup whipping cream

½ teaspoon Truvia

1/8 teaspoon orange flavor

1 cup of mixed berries

Directions:

Preheat oven to 350° F.

Using a sharp knife, divide the lemon cake into small cubes.

Dice the strawberries.

Combine the whipping cream, Truvia, and orange flavor.

Layer the fruit, cake and cream in a glass.

Serve and Enjoy!

Coconut Brownies

Ready about in: 15 min | Servings: 8 | Normal

Ingredients

½ cup coconut oil

2 ounce dark chocolate

1 cup sugar

2 ½ tablespoon water

4 whisked eggs

¼ teaspoon ground cinnamon

½ teaspoon ground anise star

¼ teaspoon coconut extract

½ teaspoon vanilla extract

1 tablespoon honey

½ cup flour

½ cup desiccated coconut

sugar, to dust

Directions:

Melt the coconut oil and dark chocolate in the microwave.

Combine with the Sugar, water, eggs, cinnamon, anise, coconut extract, vanilla, and honey in a large bowl.

Stir in the flour and desiccated coconut. Incorporate everything well.

Lightly grease a baking dish with butter. Transfer the mixture to the dish. Place the dish in the Air Fryer and bake at 355° F for 15 minutes. Remove from the Fryer and allow to cool slightly.

Take care when taking it out of the baking dish. Slice it into squares. Dust with Sugar before serving.

Chocolate Pudding

Ready about in: 50 min | Servings: 1 | Easy

Ingredients

3 tablespoon chia seeds

1 cup unsweetened milk

1 scoop cocoa powder

¼ cup fresh raspberries

½ teaspoon honey

Directions:

Mix together all of the ingredients in a large bowl.

Let rest for 15 minutes but stir halfway through.

Stir again and refrigerate for 30 minutes.

Garnish with raspberries.

Serve!

Coconut Pillow

Ready about in: 1-2 days | Servings: 4 | Normal

Ingredients

1 can unsweetened coconut milk

Berries of choice

Dark chocolate

Directions:

Refrigerate the coconut milk for 24 hours.

Remove it from your refrigerator and whip for 2-3 minutes.

Fold in the berries.

Season with the chocolate shavings.

Serve!

Coconut 'n Almond Fat Bombs

Ready about in: 15 min | Serves 12 | Normal

Ingredients

¼ cup almond flour

½ cup shredded coconut

1 tablespoon coconut oil

1 tablespoon vanilla extract

2 tablespoons liquid stevia

3 egg whites

Directions:

Select bake mode the set the temperature to preheat the Air Fryer for 5 minutes.

Combine all ingredients in a mixing bowl.

Form small balls using your hands.

Place in the Air Fryer basket and cook for 15 minutes at 400° F.

When the timer reaches 0, then press the cancel button

Serve and Enjoy

Kiwi Chocolate Cake

Ready about in: 30 min | Servings: 10 | Easy

Ingredients

1 stick softened butter

½ cup sugar

1 egg

4 Kiwi

2 tablespoons maple syrup

2 cups flour

¼ teaspoon anise star, ground

¼ teaspoon ground mace

¼ teaspoon ground cinnamon

¼ teaspoon crystallized ginger

½ teaspoon vanilla paste

Pinch of kosher salt

½ cup cocoa powder

Directions:

Beat together the softened butter and Sugar to combine well.

Mix together the egg, kiwi and maple syrup using a whisk. Combine the two mixtures, stirring well until pale and creamy. Add in the flour, anise star, mace, cinnamon, crystallized ginger, vanilla paste, salt, and cocoa powder. Mix well to form the batter. Grease 2 cake pans with cooking spray.

Transfer the batter into the cake pans and place them in the Air Fryer. Cook at 330° F for 30 minutes. Frost with chocolate glaze if desired Serve and Enjoy!

Lemon Butter Pound Cake

Ready about in: 2 hours 20 min | Servings: 8 | Easy

Ingredients

1 stick softened butter

1 cup sugar

1 medium egg

1 ¼ cups flour

1 teaspoon butter flavoring

1 teaspoon vanilla essence

Pinch of salt

¾ cup milk

Grated zest of 1 medium-sized lemon

For the Glaze:

2 tablespoons freshly squeezed lemon juice

Directions:

In a large bowl, use a creamer to mix together the butter and Sugar. Fold in the egg and continue to stir.

Add in the flour, butter flavoring, vanilla essence, and salt, combining everything well.

Pour in the milk, followed by the lemon zest, and continue to mix.

Lightly brush the inside of a cake pan with the melted butter.

Pour the cake batter into the cake pan.

Place the pan in the Air Fryer and bake at 350° F for 15 minutes.

After removing it from the Fryer, run a knife around the edges of the cake to loosen it from the pan and transfer it to a serving plate.

Leave it to cool completely.

In the meantime, make the glaze by combining with the lemon juice. Pour the glaze over the cake and let it sit for a further 2 hours before serving.

Chocolate Chip Cookies

Ready about in: 25 min | Servings: 9 | Normal

Ingredients

1 ¼ cup flour

2/3 cup chocolate chips, or any kind of baker's chocolate

⅓ cup sugar

½ cup butter

4 tablespoons honey

1 tablespoons milk

High quality cooking spray

Directions:

Set your Air Fryer to 320° F and allow to warm up for about 10 minutes.

In the meantime, in a large bowl, cream the butter to soften it.

Add in the Sugar and combine to form a light and fluffy consistency. Stir in the honey.

Gradually fold in the flour, incorporating it well.

Using baker's chocolate, use a rolling pin or a mallet to break it up and create chocolate chips.

Throw the chocolate into the bowl and mix well to ensure the chips are evenly distributed throughout the dough.

Finally, add in the milk and combine well.

Lightly spritz your Air Fryer basket with the cooking spray.

Transfer the cookie dough into the Fryer and cook for 20 minutes.

Slice into 9 cookies. Serve immediately. Alternatively, the cookies can be stored in an airtight container for up to 3 days.

Mini Strawberry Pies

Ready about in: 15 min | Servings: 8 | Normal

Ingredients

1 cup sugar

¼ teaspoon ground cloves

1/8 teaspoon cinnamon powder

1 teaspoon vanilla extract

1 [12-ounce] biscuit dough

12 ounce strawberry pie filling

¼ cup butter, melted

Directions:

In a bowl, mix together the Sugar, cloves, cinnamon, and vanilla.

With a rolling pin, roll each piece of the biscuit dough into a flat, round circle.

Spoon an equal amount of the strawberry pie filling onto the center of each biscuit.

Roll up the dough. Dip the biscuits into the melted butter and coat them with the sugar mixture.

Coat with a light brushing of non-stick cooking spray on all sides.

Transfer the cookies to the Air Fryer and bake them at 340° F for roughly 10 minutes, or until a golden-brown color is achieved.

Allow cooling for 5 minutes before serving.

Banana Walnut Bread

Ready about in: 40 min | Servings: 1 | Easy

Ingredients

7 ounce flour

¼ teaspoon baking powder

2.5 ounce butter

5.5 ounce sugar

2 medium eggs

14 ounce bananas, peeled

2.8 ounce chopped walnuts

Directions:

Select bake mode the set the temperature to preheat the Air Fryer to 350° F.

Take a baking tin small enough to fit inside the Air Fryer and grease the inside with butter.

Mix together the flour and the baking powder in a bowl.

In a separate bowl, beat together the Sugar and butter until fluffy and pale. Gradually add in the flour and egg. Stir.

Throw in the walnuts and combine again.

Mash the bananas using a fork and transfer them to the bowl. Mix once more, until everything is incorporated.

Pour the mixture into the tin, place inside the Fryer and cook for 10 minutes.

Serve and Enjoy

Oatmeal Apple & Plum Crumble

Ready about in: 20 min | Servings: 6 | Easy

Ingredients

¼ lb. plums, pitted and chopped

¼ lb. Braeburn apples, cored and chopped

1 tablespoons fresh lemon juice

2 ½ ounce sugar

1 tablespoons honey

½ teaspoon ground mace

½ teaspoon vanilla paste

1 cup fresh cranberries

⅓ cup oats

2/3 cup flour

½ stick butter, chilled

1 tablespoons cold water

Directions:

Coat the plums and apples with lemon juice, Sugar, honey, and ground mace.

Lightly coat the inside of a cake pan with cooking spray.

Pour the fruit mixture into the pan.

In a bowl, mix together all of the other ingredients, combining everything well.

Use a palette knife to spread this mixture evenly over the fruit.

Place the pan in the Air Fryer and air bake at 390° F for 20 minutes.

Ensure the crumble is cooked through before serving.

Banana & Vanilla Pastry Puffs

Ready about in: 15 minutes | Servings: 8 | Normal

Ingredients

1 package [8-ounce] crescent dinner rolls, refrigerated

1 cup milk

4 ounce instant vanilla pudding

4 ounce cream cheese, softened

2 bananas, peeled and sliced

1 egg, lightly beaten

Directions:

Roll out the crescent dinner rolls and slice each one into 8 squares.

Mix together the milk, pudding, and cream cheese using a whisk.

Scoop equal amounts of the mixture into the pastry squares. Add the banana slices on top.

Fold the squares around the filling, pressing down on the edges to seal them.

Apply a light brushing of the egg to each pastry puff before placing them in the Air Fryer.

Air bake at 355° F for 10 minutes.

When the timer reaches 0, then press the cancel button

Serve and Enjoy!

Choco-Coconut Puddin

Ready about in: 65 min | Servings: 1 | Easy

Ingredients

1 cup coconut milk

2 tablespoons cacao powder or organic cocoa

½ teaspoon Sugar powder extract or 2 tablespoons honey/maple syrup

½ tablespoons quality gelatin

1 tablespoons water

Directions:

On medium heat, combine the coconut milk, cocoa and sweetener.

In a separate bowl, mix in the gelatin and water.

Add to the pan and stir until fully dissolved.

Pour into small dishes and refrigerate for 1 hour.

Serve and Enjoy!

Milton Keynes UK
Ingram Content Group UK Ltd.
UKHW022246050124
435571UK00004B/147

9 781802 601794